THE STILL VOICE

Other books of White Eagle's teaching

THE STILL VOICE

*A White Eagle book
of meditation*

**THE WHITE EAGLE
PUBLISHING TRUST**
NEW LANDS · LISS · HAMPSHIRE

British Library Cataloguing in Publication Data
White Eagle (*Spirit*)
The still voice.
1. Meditation – Addresses, essays, lectures
I. Title   II. Cooke, Grace
131   BL627
ISBN 0–85487–049–0

Set in 11 on 14 point Linotron Janson
by King's English Typesetters Ltd., Cambridge,
and Printed in Great Britain
by Fletcher & Son Ltd., Norwich

CONTENTS

INTRODUCTION

JESUS said, *The kingdom of God is within you*; and he told us, further, *Seek ye first the kingdom of God*. Through the ages men have sought and found this inner kingdom of happiness through some form of meditation. As they have withdrawn the consciousness from the outer, everyday world, with its cares and problems and weaknesses, into the stillness and purity of the world within, they have found what can only be described as a living spring of light and joy from which they have been able to draw strength and wisdom for each day. It is the well-spring of love, too, and constant meditation within this still temple of the heart can stimulate all that is good and loving in the soul, and bring, in the end, health and harmony to the physical body.

This living spring is really the Christ

which is in each one of us. As White Eagle says elsewhere in this book, 'Through meditation and quiet contemplation the outer layers of the mind and emotion are gradually laid aside and man rests in the innermost place of stillness where the jewel of truth lies, the jewel within the lotus of his heart. This is the light which lighteth every man, the Christ the Son of God in him . . . The mind must be stilled, and the spirit must become aware, must become conscious of its being. Then the soul of man becomes illumined with divine spirit and consciousness expands into worlds of beauty and truth which bring peace and joy to the human soul.'

In White Eagle's method of creative meditation we are taught to use what he describes as the higher, creative, mind, to visualise or create symbols of beauty which help us to still the busy mind and withdraw the consciousness from outward form to the inner reality of the spirit, to utter stillness and awareness of God. The soul's guidance which comes as a result of this awareness can convey itself to the conscious mind through spiritual visions, and often does so, but not always. It can be just an inner knowing, a radiance, a feeling of intense joy or all-embracing love. Indeed it may not become apparent during the meditation period at all but will manifest later in a new strength and a new wisdom to deal with the problems of daily life.

In this little book we have collected some of White Eagle's guiding wisdom for every day, and have added short meditations, often given by White Eagle himself, to help the aspirant on this journey inward to the world of light.* It should be emphasised that the symbols given are not the end in itself, but the 'way in', which can lead to unfolding vision and deep spiritual experience. Hold the picture given for as long as you can. Let it become alive and real for

* One of the readings appeared formerly in the White Eagle book, PRAYER IN THE NEW AGE. We have included it because it seemed useful in the present context.

you, growing in intensity and radiance as you gaze upon it. Let it bring utter stillness to your mind and soul.

Some Practical Suggestions

Deep stillness of mind and heart and resultant spiritual awareness only come after much patient endeavour – or, as White Eagle would say, 'keeping on keeping on' on the spiritual path.

The aspirant can be helped by certain simple rituals. It is good, for instance, to keep to the same time for the daily meditation practice – early morning is suggested, for the mental world is quiet then; and the morning meditation can irradiate the whole day. Meditate if possible in a quiet, prepared place; and ideally, always use the same chair. This is because the chair and the place become associated with the meditative state; they begin to acquire an aura of quietness which in itself becomes a protection from the busy-ness of the world. The chair should be comfortable and upright so that the body can be held poised and erect, spine straight, without strain or tension in any part of the body. A simple way of relaxing the shoulders and the back of the neck, where so much tension is centred, is to shrug the shoulders once or twice and then try to feel their weight and the weight of the arms; also to let the head drop forward and feel its weight and the stretch at the back of the neck, before gently straightening again. The ankles should be crossed, right over left, and the hands lie cupped in the lap, left in right, in a relaxed attitude of quiet surrender and waiting upon God. The whole body is poised yet relaxed, at peace yet alert.

Now, begin to breathe a little more deeply, a little more slowly, but quietly and gently, without strain, listening to the quiet rhythm of your own breathing. As you do this the active mind begins to become still and the consciousness is slowly withdrawn from the outer to the inner world of stillness and meditation.

Each will find his own way of using the passages in this book to his own best advantage, but it is suggested that it might be helpful to memorise, in essence if not in detail, the picture given for meditation (it appears in italic in the text) so that the consciousness, once withdrawn, does not have to return to the printed page but can remain centred within.

The return from the deep inner awareness to consciousness of the everyday world should be slow and deliberate, perhaps through picturing a beautiful garden and resting there for a while amid the perfect beauty and colour of the world of nature. Then again use the breath to help bring you 'back to earth'; breathe deeply and strongly, and as you gradually and deliberately become conscious of the physical body feel that with each breath the body is becoming filled with light. In imagination see the brow, throat, heart and solar plexus centre 'sealed' with the cross of light within the circle of light, and see the whole body encircled by a ring of light.

Some of the meditation passages end with an affirmation which, spoken with conviction, aloud or quietly in the heart before returning into the world (and, indeed, used many times a day) can help to build light and health into the body, and to strengthen the soul's link with the shining, celestial self in the world of light, which we all have.

White Eagle himself, our gentle brother of the spirit, speaks to us from this world of light. We pray that this little book, with White Eagle's loving wise guidance will help you in your soul's quest and become your friend and constant companion 'in the hours of meditation'.

THE JEWEL IN THE LOTUS

WHEN a man can consciously contact the true Source of his being, the true Source of his life, power flows into him and shines through him, harmony enters into his life and gives him a new outlook, so that those things which once upset and hurt him no longer affect the peace of his heart. Usually man is filled with conflict, but if he can withdraw from all those difficult conditions which bind him and seek the Source of harmony within himself, the lifestream from God pours through him, and his material conditions are gradually and surely brought into harmony. All wrongs are righted when the consciousness of God is alive in the heart.

Through meditation and quiet contemplation the outer layers of the mind and emotion are gradually laid aside and man rests in the innermost place of stillness where the jewel of truth lies, the jewel within the lotus of his heart. This is the light which lighteth every man, the Christ the Son of God in him. Search for it, my brethren, but not with a great deal of noise and talk; just quietly keep on keeping on, searching in the stillness of your own innermost being. The mind must be stilled, and the spirit must become aware, must become conscious of its being. Then the soul of man becomes illumined with the divine spirit and consciousness expands into worlds of beauty and truth which bring peace and joy to the human soul.

I am the way, the truth, and the life: no man cometh unto the Father, but by me. No man cometh into the kingdom of heaven, except through the spirit of the gentle Christ, the glorious Son of God in man.

*

To start your meditation, breathe gently, deeply, rhythmically, and think of the golden sunlight of God filling your whole being . . .

Now visualise the infinite and eternal garden, so quiet, yet sunlit and full of life . . . see the still pool, and floating on the shining water the pure white lily. Gaze upon this perfect flower and into the golden light in the centre, the blazing jewel . . . Become the jewel, enfolded by the pure white petals of the lotus.

I am in the Light . . . I AM the Light . . . I bless and raise all men into the Light.

THE SERVICE OF LOVE

WE KNOW that the one wish and aspiration of your heart is that you may serve humanity. This you cannot fail to do if you send forth love. This does not mean only where you choose, but at every moment of life . . . Love: love life, love all the blessings that are yours; live to love, love to live, thinking not of self, thinking only of the great Self, which is universal brotherhood. Understanding of the mysteries of the spirit will first bring you consciousness of your at-one-ment with every form of life; it will bring love without limitation.

When suffering comes, cleanse and purify your thinking by the love of Christ. In other words, do not dwell on the injury; do not allow self-pity to possess your mind; but go into the Lodge of your own inner being, close the door, and raise your aspirations to the blazing Star, to the Great White Light of your life, Christ, the Son of God. He will heal your sorrow; bitterness will fall away; it will be melted, consumed in the fire of the love of Christ.

The only reality is God. You are in the heart of God.

*

Visualise the still white flame; hold it very still before you, as you breathe gently and quietly. Let no breath or thought give movement to the flame. Then, see that still flame in the centre of the Star (or Sun) . . . Know that this little flame is the God in you, your spirit, part of the great Sun. Let the brightness of the flame draw you into the heart of the Sun . . .

GOD IN MAN

YOU enjoy the sunshine and the flowers, and the birds; you rejoice in the glory of the skies, the blessing of the raindrops, the reflection of God's beauty in the water and in all that grows on earth. But in man himself you will see the highest manifestation of the love of the Father. Can you conceive anything more beautiful than the human life of the Master, so gentle and loving, giving without reservation to his brethren on earth?

O beloved children, follow the way of the gentle Master of love, the Son of God, for he is truly the saviour of mankind. The wise man knows that of himself he is nothing, that of himself he can do nothing; but the Christ which dwelleth in him doeth all things, and will draw all men unto Him.

I am the way, the truth and the life: no man cometh unto the Father, but by me – through love; this is the law. Beloved children, when you enter into communion with God and with the Master, you raise your consciousness to the highest plane of spiritual life.

In each man there is a permanent atom, the permanent part of his nature, which lives in heaven with God. Few are sufficiently evolved yet to contact that permanent atom consciously whilst living in the flesh. But you can, if you will, touch that plane of light and love, and can function consciously from that temple which is your eternal home.

*

Picture now the gentle human figure of the Great Healer, all love. He bids us follow him and he leads us to the heights, into the temple of the Sun – it is as though we are absorbed into the Sun . . . Gradually we become aware of great beings of the Sun, the Christ–Star-circle, who hold the earth and all her people in their care.

Say to yourself, 'I am a flame in the heart of the Sun. I am in the heart of the Sun'.

4

GOD IS LAW, BUT GOD IS ALSO LOVE

WE WOULD bring you a keener awareness of the immortal truth that you live and can only live because you are a son or daughter of God. You are a seed of God, born from His heart. Try to remember your relationship to this divine Love and Wisdom which is your Creator. Not only is God the scientific law which controls all life and keeps the stars and planets in their courses, God is also of humanity. He understands your heart and your need. Never think of God as a remote power watching the follies of mankind from afar. God is law, but God is also love. Live every day, every minute of your life conscious that you are living in God, in the heavenly state of love; and that all creatures are of

God, and belong to this one universal life from which no tiny part can be separated. All are one in this divine Spirit.

*

Visualise now the temple of the Star in the world of spirit. It is built of spiritual substance, transparent, pulsating with life and colour like dancing sunlight.

And in the temple there is deep stillness, a silence which is of eternity, infinity.

To enter into this temple and this silence is to become part of the whole, one with all life, in the heart of the Solar Logos . . .

9

THE LIFE THAT MAKES ALL THINGS NEW

AS YOU accept with patience and sweet surrender the difficulties you encounter, so will you find flowing into you a light and a life-force which will make all things new. This comes to a man or woman by degrees, very simply at first, very quietly; occasionally you become aware of a glow in your heart, aware of a harmony which is shaping your life anew. If you direct the right thought to those around you; and if you put into action the law of love in the face of any adverse circumstances in which you find yourself, you will find that these circumstances will gradually smooth themselves out, events will start to work more harmoniously for you, and then you will say, 'God is very good to me'. You will be beginning to realise that outside your own effort there is a power, a love, which is helping actively, bringing you inward peace and happiness.

This glow in your heart which brings such sweet happiness may remain for a few minutes, a few hours, or a few days – and then disappear; but by degrees it will increase in you. As life advances you will experience it more often; for you are moving forward up a spiral of light which will eventually bring you, a true son–daughter of God, to the kingdom of eternal light.

*

Meditate on the symbol of the soft pink rose. You are not looking on it from afar, as something outside yourself. It is in your heart, softly glowing, the petals gently opening to receive the golden warmth of the sunshine from above. There is a light from the heart of the rose too. The light from above and the light in the heart of the rose blend as one . . .

11

THE WAY TO HAPPINESS

HAPPINESS is a religion; and it is good for brothers to expect happiness, to endeavour to create and share happiness. God created you to be happy. And so the purpose of all the teaching which comes to us from the Brotherhood above, is to point the way to happiness.

The question will arise immediately as to the meaning of the cross, and why man has suffered and why you feel unhappy. Rightly viewed, the way of the cross is the path to liberation; it is the way to life. Think of the cross not as a symbol of suffering, but of renunciation, surrender, a giving up of the self-will to the will of God. With this renunciation there comes such a calm peaceful joy, a realisation that all is well. God in His infinite love knows your heart and is giving back to you one hundred-fold all that you have surrendered.

You may rest quietly, knowing that the wise Mother and the infinitely loving Father are both bringing the children of the present age through the weakness of self-will to the sunlight of happiness and goodwill and brotherhood, to the perfect life which is prepared for all God's family.

*

Withdraw now into the sunlit garden of the spirit. Picture the sunlight dancing on the moving stream, and feel the joy of this dancing light. See, now, as the Sun plays upon the spray, all the colours of a beautiful rainbow. And in the rainbow, the young and joyous form of the Master Jesus appears. He calls you to walk with him in the garden, and you walk there with him.

LOOK UP INTO THE SUN

TAKE little notice of passing difficulties and obstacles. Keep on keeping on steadily. There are forces which would buffet and confuse you, but you will overcome these forces by steadily looking up towards the Christ. Look up into the Sun, to the point of light in the heart of the Sun.

Surrender to divine wisdom, knowing that what is happening to you is an opportunity to grow in love, to draw closer to divine love. Do not think of life in the physical body as being the only life. Think of life as being eternal, and of yourself as a tiny spark of that divine life, one day to return to the heart of the Sun. You, the child of God, are learning to walk a path which is leading you back to your heavenly parents. This is the goal of your life –

conscious union with God, divine love and wisdom, peace, and joy.

The secret, when you are feeling hurt and disappointed with yourself, or with circumstances, or with your brother man, is to learn to rise in thought to God, and say: 'Thou art all wisdom and love. Thou knowest my soul's need. I resign my life to Thee.'

*

Now, we would draw you all into the great Heart; you are children of God and all good flows from God.

For one quiet moment, try to use the power of thought and imagination to visualise the form of Christ, the Son, the Golden One, all love. See Him robed in the light of the Sun, radiating love for all mankind. Be still . . . you are in Him . . . He is in you. You are nothing, yet everything.

Peace be with you. All is well when you dwell at peace within God's heart, and feel God within your own heart as a quickening presence, as living warmth and comfort.

THE DIVINE FIRE

YOU are a son of God in embryo, and as you endeavour to love and to serve, to be compassionate, tolerant, and patient, and to follow in humility the example of Jesus through the Christ in him, so you will grow and develop the solar body, the body of the Sun, the body of the Christos. Do the work of healing with your heart and soul and mind, saying always: *Not I but the Father that dwelleth in me, he doeth the works.* God the Father does the work – the son is the receptacle.

The magic white light of the spirit is within your breast, and in this white light lies the power of all spiritual work, of all service to the world. Spiritual work spreads over the whole earth not only through words but through the Christ-life, the

Christ-love in every human soul. This divine fire must be brought into operation in each brother and each sister so that the light blazes and dispels all darkness, consumes all evil, overcomes the power of darkness. With every breath you take breathe forth the light: with every word you utter give forth the vibration of light and truth. May the temple within your heart be guarded by angels of light.

*

Picture now a sparkling flashing jewel, like a diamond, every facet a blaze of colour, reflecting light . . . Gradually, as you gaze upon this flashing jewel, you become absorbed into it and the ray of light from above which is reflected from the jewel is shining into your heart. You are caught up into the great Star, at one with the shining brothers who in perfect harmony and utter stillness are meditating, and radiating the light of the Christ love into the world.

Breathe in the breath of God, and breathe out the blessing of love and healing upon the earth.

17

SERVICE OF THE LIGHT

YOU ask us, 'White Eagle, what can we do to help mankind?' And we answer:

By daily, hourly, every moment of your life endeavouring to realise your true self, which lies buried deep in your innermost being. It will rise in you like a stream of light on which you will be able to rise to a higher level of consciousness where you will find yourself enveloped in the power and love of God.

Practise this daily realisation of the Great White Light within your own being and project it forth into the world of men. Then, my friends, the mists around the earth will be dispelled. Do not look to others to do the work for you. Every man is his own saviour; and every man is the saviour of all mankind.

Apply spiritual light and truth and love to your every action. Pray that the will of God may become manifest through you and in your life.

Let your brotherhood be not merely lip-service but brotherhood active and heartfelt in the smallest detail. You will have no need to worry then about the events which lie ahead. You can meet them with confidence and hope. You can be certain that you, a unit, are helping all mankind, for as part of the whole you can raise all people to receive succour from God.

The love of the Brotherhood is ever with you. Look to the light of the Star: it will never fail you.

*

Be still, within the temple of your innermost being . . . and there, on the altar of light, see the chalice of sparkling crystal, perfect in form. It is the chalice of your heart. Lift it in worship, to be filled with the great light from God, the living wine of the spirit; filled, that others too may drink from the cup.

19

THE HEALING POWER
OF LOVE

WE COME to help you to attune yourselves to the infinite power of love. Love is
the worker of miracles, divine love will
meet every need of your life. The material
world and your imprisonment in the physical body may seem to you very hard, and
you have become accustomed to thinking in
terms of pain and inconvenience and ills of
the flesh which seem so obstinate and will
not be removed. Of course they will not, if
you think about them; but as soon as you
dwell in spirit, attuned to the love of your
Father–Mother God and Christ the Son,
you will feel the inflow of a magic power of
healing. But don't be in too much of a
hurry. Be patient.

If you will train yourselves to think in

terms of love every moment of life you will find that unconsciously and almost imperceptibly a beautiful healing will take place in your life.

There are many methods of healing but only one true source from which all healing flows, and this source is divine love – the foundation of all life. The Master Jesus is at the head of the healing ray, and it is his special work to help humanity to make contact with the Source of life. He comes to you whenever you truly call. No prayer goes unanswered, because true prayer sets up a vibration in your soul which goes right to the Source. True prayer is the complete surrender of the soul to God's will. 'Thy will be done in earth. Thy will be done in my physical body. Thy will be done in me.' God's will is good, and His will is that your body should be healthy, holy and able to enjoy all the beauty of life. May the wisdom which will guide you to this end fill your heart and mind.

*

Now will you be still, very still, and visualise the presence of the Christ, a radiant personality with love shining from Him . . . He stands in a pure white pulsating light, and from Him the rays are now penetrating your heart . . .

In love, my child, there is no separation . . . All are together one in God, in the consciousness of eternal life. There is no past, no future, all is in the eternal Now.

I live and have my being in the eternal life, in God.

THE JOURNEY OF LIFE

THE PATH of life on which you have set your feet is high and steep but it is not unconquerable. Many have climbed this path before you, some are half-way up, some are right at the top, but those who are at the top are not unmindful of you and your efforts. They come unseen, unheard, to give you strength, to give you light, to enfold you in their love.

The work of man on earth is to learn how to manifest the love and the beauty of God. And these companions of your spirit whom you have known in former lives are with you to help you. They guide you and help you to learn your lessons; they are with you in sorrow and perplexity to strengthen you and in joy to help you to be happy.

Each time you are tempted to resort to

the weakness and error of the lower mind and of the material world, but instead of being overcome by these temptations of the lower self you respond to the light of the higher self, or to the prompting of your guide, who fills your being with love and humility, so you grow stronger, you take a step forward and upward towards your goal.

Yet still the journey seems long and you become discouraged, and begin to think you will never reach the golden heaven. We know, my children, we know; but we come to bring you good cheer, for joy must be your companion on this path leading to the heart of the Father. We understand the weariness of the flesh, we understand the soul-weariness, but we know too that there comes without fail a sustaining, refreshing grace to uphold the weary traveller on his journey.

We bring you a message, not only of joy and hope, but of assurance that God's love is omnipotent, omniscient, omnipresent;

and it is for you to receive it as a welcome and honoured guest, into your heart.

*

Withdraw, now, from the senses of the outer world and come into the sunlit garden within. Here, in the infinite and eternal garden of the spirit, is a stream of crystal, sparkling water.

Listen to the music of the moving water and all the sounds of nature in this springtime garden . . . See the sunlight dancing on the water.

Your guide is with you and offers you a cup of crystal water from the stream. It is cool and cleansing, life giving . . . you drink and are refreshed.

12

PRAY THAT YOU MAY BE MASTER

WE WOULD convey to your hearts the truth of the power of love; but you can prove it for yourselves if you will put the law into operation in your own life. This you are all endeavouring to do except when you become overdriven and disturbed by little things, by petty things. Yet you have latent within you all the attributes of a master and must learn to rule your lodge with love and truth, wisdom and beauty. Pray that you may be the master in the lodge of your own being.

The power of the master in you is the power of love. Love has been the power of the Brotherhood all down the ages. Brothers have always been gentle and loving and pure, but the emanation from them has been so powerful that it has held this planet on its course, and within the power of the light.

Man, through self-will, has departed from the simple life of love, with the result that there is darkness over the face of the earth. But Christ still lives within the darkness, and according to your individual effort, so the light of the Star will turn all darkness into light – light will absorb all the darkness. But it is through constant life and work of every gentle brother that this will take place.

*

Forget all the conflict on the earth; open your heart and follow the guide of your spirit into the golden world above, into the sunlit garden, the eternal and infinite garden . . .

Walk in this garden with joy in your heart, and see the shining faces and feel the gentle companionship of the brothers of the Star.

See the animals of all kinds in their natural

state, just see the gentleness of these animals . . .

You find yourself, now, in the rose garden. You inhale the perfume of the roses, and choosing one rose imagine yourself going right into the very centre, that golden centre of that pure golden rose . . .

Your rose has become a golden temple and the petals of the rose are the angels all around you. Worship the Golden One, in this temple of the living rose.

13

BE OF GOOD HEART

REMEMBER to enter the silence when your need is great; so few of our earthly brothers seem able to do this. They have a great urge to do something on the physical plane when in trouble; yet the most valuable thing you can do is to be still and seek God within. When in doubt, do nothing, be still.

Certain lessons can only be learnt in the physical life. The elder brethren have only one hope and wish, and this is to help their earthly brethren towards the great surrender to the beauty and love and glory of the Creator, the Great White Spirit. Although we are able to bring you help when you call for it, when it is asked for selflessly, it is no part of the work of the invisible Brotherhood to make your path too easy, nor to prevent you from learning valuable lessons, which, when learnt, enable you to enter into the full joy of accomplishment, and expansion of spiritual vision and consciousness.

So we say to you, be of good heart, be simple in faith, surrender all care and burdens to the spiritual love which watches over and directs the life of every child of the light. Do not be impatient or anxious. The light will bring into manifestation on earth all that is good for you in God's sight.

Within the silence is the heart of truth. Be still . . . and you will know no fear. Be still . . . and you will know the radiance of health in your soul. Be still . . . and you will know the Power which has created you.

*

Now, rise in spirit to the mountain top and see the Sun on the horizon. As it gradually rises in the heavens you see it is reflected in the still waters of a lake, high in the mountains.

You worship the Great Spirit manifesting in that golden radiance, and as you do so you traverse the path of light across the waters, right into the heart of the Sun temple, and kneel in silence before the Christ-being . . . You know eternal peace and at-one-ment.

14

YOU ARE IMMORTAL SPIRIT

WE COME to help you to break your bonds, to liberate yourselves from the earth's limitations and dis-ease.

Keep in your hearts, like a shining jewel, the presence of God, and share this presence with those about you.

We know that this is not easy; we know your individual difficulties and needs; but we ask you to make every effort to rise above the temptations of self-pity and desire. Remember that God knows what is good for your spiritual unfoldment and your ultimate happiness. Each hour, each day, each week that you maintain your inner poise and strength of purpose, brings in time release from your desires. As the light and love of God within your life increase, so that which formerly hurt you has no more power. Do not seek for the satisfaction of your desires, nor balm for your self-pity. Be free, and happy in the life God has given you. You are spirit, you are immortal, you are radiant beings, children of God, free in God's life. Live in your spirit and allow nothing to bind or limit your spirit.

*

Rise in imagination above the limitation and darkness of the earth, into the light of the Sun. Imagine the glorious Sun in the heavens above. Breathe deeply, absorbing the golden light and warmth into your being. It is power, it is life, it can recreate you on every plane of your being. The creative power, this mighty Presence, can and will banish and consume all inharmony.

Say to yourself, 'God is in me – divine light floods and fills every atom of my being'.

15

THE GIFT OF UNDERSTANDING

YOU SEEK for knowledge, you seek for understanding. You will not find it in books but in the universe, in life, through reading men's hearts with tender love; through surrendering to the gentle ever-growing light of Christ in the heart.

You can pray for no more precious gift than understanding, for when understanding comes there is no more condemnation, nor harsh judgment, but ever-growing love.

All men consciously or unconsciously are seeking understanding of God's laws, understanding of God's love, and of the mystery of man's own complex nature. At whatever stage we have reached on the evolutionary path, we still see before us further golden peaks to climb. Life is ever unfolding, and as the vision unfolds understanding comes.

Never pass judgment on another, for you cannot see the whole picture, and if you could see, then you would not judge. If you continually look to the gentle love of the Christ-heart you will judge only yourself.

Gentleness, kindness, patience is the way. Know that in every individual soul, both on earth and out of the earth-body, dwells the divine light, the Christ in embryo, waiting to come forth, and you and we can bring it forth. We can assist in the birth of Christ.

*

We give you a vision now of our brethren, your brethren, kneeling round the altar in the temple of the Star. With hands together, uplifted, they are worshipping the ever-growing light of the jewel within the lotus . . . In this jewel, lying so pure and still in the lotus of the heart, you will learn to read all wisdom. You will learn to go direct to the jewel, and there, in a timeless flash, you will comprehend truth, not with the mind but with the heart.

16

THE MIND IN THE HEART

IN THE spirit world is a beautiful garden, and everything which grows therein is an expression of the spirit of God; the flowers and trees, their colouring and perfume, the song of the birds and the play of the fountains, the layout of the garden itself, are all manifestations of the highest and purest Godlike thought. Angels help to create this garden. In the centre of the garden is a lake of crystal water reflecting the sky and the flowers and trees, and the reflection makes the garden even lovelier. As the garden is reflected in the still waters of the lake, so is truth reflected in the heart of man. But to reflect truth, the heart must be tranquil, serene and still.

The mind of itself cannot understand or know truth, for the mind is so often a turbulent sea at the mercy of the emotions, the likes, the dislikes and the passions of life. The mind can be as an arrogant dictator seeing no wrong in itself. Truth can only reflect in such a mind in broken fragments; this is why earthly people fail to understand the plan of God in the world.

But the mind of the heart, like the still pool at the centre of the garden, reflects pure truth from the mind of God. Man can look into the pool and see the law of cause and effect at work, can see the reason for all that happens and the perfection of God's plan for the ultimate good and progress of all mankind.

Standing by this lake and watching the reflection of goodness and beauty, man sees his own reflection too; he sees himself as he is, in comparison with the beauty and glory of God and the manifestation of God's truth. And then he gains the jewel of truth . . .

*

Meditate on the infinite and eternal garden of the spirit. Be still, beside the lake of peace . . .

See how perfectly all the beauties of the garden are reflected in the still water. Be still . . . and gradually you become aware of the reflection in the waters of the perfect six-pointed Star, and as you gaze, the Star becomes the form of the Shining One. He–She is by your side . . . You meditate together beside the blue lake of peace.

17

BE CALM, BE STEADFAST

WHEN you try to do things, and they will not go the way you want, leave them alone. Do not try to force things the way *you* would like them to go. Just leave them alone. Do your best, obey the law of love, and you will be surprised at how circumstances will work out far better for you than if you had had your own way. Let God have His way, and you just be patient and wait.

Be calm, steadfast and peaceful. Accept things as they come and do not be rushed into wrong decisions or overcome by the forces of ignorance. Be steadfast, with a quiet, inner, peaceful and persistent knowing that the Great Architect of the Universe holds the plan of your life in His hands.

The Star is not only a great cosmic

power, it is also a tender, loving, guiding power, a protecting power in your own lives. If you can surrender yourselves to the sweet and lovely Star radiance, you will find that your pathway will be one of light and happiness and gentle peace.

Nothing matters more than this spiritual life in you. It is the key into heaven – heaven on earth as well as the heaven world after death.

*

Picture the shining six-pointed Star, and as you breathe in imagine that you are being filled with God's light, love and strength which is pouring down on you from the Star. You are bathed in light. The Star is just above your head and the rays from it, as they pour down through your head and into your whole being, form a great protective cone of light in which you are held serene and secure.

18

THE SOUND IN THE SILENCE

THERE comes a time when you seek to comprehend the true meaning of peace, and how you as an individual may find that peace, a peace which the world can neither give you nor take from you.

This is the way. Visualise the blazing Star, still, and yet full of life and light. Identify yourselves with the Star, with the centre of that Star. In your imagination go right into the still centre of that Star, and in the centre you will find that all the anxieties of the material life, all the struggle that you encounter in daily life, will all fall away from you. In the heart of the Star is deep, eternal peace, and in this peace you are united with all whom you love.

Give yourselves time daily to remember this Star temple, and go into it, away from

the noise and turmoil and tumult, the fears
and anxieties of the material plane. And
there in the inner, inner Star, find divine,
holy peace. Hear in your soul the music of
Christ, the music of the spiritual spheres,
the music of the holy Word . . . the audible
lifestream which flows from the heart of the
Creator.

*

*Be still now in mind and body. Listen
inwardly. Beneath all sound, beneath all
thought, in the deep silence at the heart of
creation, you will hear the harmony of God.*

19

THE ANGEL OF PEACE

BELOVED children, we ask you to see the power of the eternal Spirit working throughout your lives. Think in terms of the smoothness of the power of God at work in your lives, in your health, in your affairs. All things are working together for good; be calm and patient. Do your best within your own capacity and see this beautiful power of love, the love of a father for his children, working through your affairs.

Whatever is placed before you in the form of tests, go calmly through and all will be well. You are on a path of ever-unfolding light and beauty and happiness. Be thankful always, be thankful to God, to the elder brethren, for their loving care of you. Out of darkness and chaos comes light. We would like you to feel this inexhaustible flow of spiritual healing, spiritual power to evolve all earthly things in a most perfect form. You have nothing to be afraid of because all your needs are supplied and all is well.

Live in the consciousness of the light, and know that all is progressing towards perfection.

You could save yourself so much pain, so much anxiety, if you would always seek for help at the spiritual level. Don't look to the material world for the guidance and direction you need, but seek always the spiritual contact, seek the place of inner peace and stillness and cultivate in yourselves a certainty of the power of God's love.

Your heavenly Father loves you and has given His angels charge over you, to care for you in all your ways . . . When you really know this, deep within, you will be at peace.

*

Meditate on the angel of Peace – so quiet and still and very powerful, but all love. Her garment is the softest blue like the sky, with a touch of rose pink and sunshine. It could almost be likened to mother-of-pearl. As you breathe in her influence all care falls away, your heart is stilled and stayed on God. As you breathe her influence out into the world turbulent emotions are stilled, a quietness comes into the hearts of men.

THE CELESTIAL SELF

MOST people think that the personality they know on this physical plane is all of them; but remember that only a very small part of you is imprisoned in physical life; what is manifesting through the body is only the point of the triangle. That small part of the whole self comes to earth as a messenger, a seeker, to gather experience in the flesh to make way for the God-consciousness to manifest through the very narrow channel which you call your personality. But God has given you the power to realise and contact that higher self.

In your meditation you know that you rise into higher planes and find yourself in a temple built of light. You find yourself before an altar where you bow in prayer, you are caught up, you are engulfed in this pure and glorious state of consciousness. This is really your celestial embodiment. The celestial body is the sum total of all the wisdom and good attained through many incarnations, and is linked with the limited personality of earth through the bright flame of the Christ spirit in the heart. Through meditation, through withdrawing into the still heart-consciousness, or higher mind, we can find and bring into operation in our outer lives the soul-wisdom garnered through the ages, the radiance and perfection of that shining celestial body.

Withdraw each day from the tumult of the outer world, and try to feel the presence of your noble heavenly self. Look to that self for your guidance and your inspiration in life; be strong and poised and true to that enduring self.

*

Come now into the infinite and eternal garden of the spirit, gaze upon the still clear water of the pool reflecting the sky, the heavens. On the surface of the pool floats the pure white lily, symbol of your own spiritual nature. See, lying in the golden heart of the lily the sparkling jewel. This is the divine life, the Christ in you, and the Sun shining upon it causes it to radiate all the colours of the rainbow. By your aspiration there grows from that lily the perfect form of the master soul, the master spirit, visualised by your soul as the Christos. Can you feel the beauty of that radiant Being who is all love . . .? And you are in that love for ever and ever and ever. Through all eternity, you, the seed of God, are in God's heart. What have you to fear? Nothing can hurt you, for you are in God.

Rest, in your innermost heart, in God.

21

THE ROSE OF LOVE

WE LOVE each one of you, and we are working to help you to grow the light within your heart. We look right into the heart and we know that every man and woman has within them the love of God. Look, my brethren, for that spark of light, of God, within your fellows, and approach that – if not verbally then in your heart. The light in the heart is pure spirit. Learn to be guided by the spirit, which is the love within you.

And remember, you do not walk the path alone. We know, more than you can yet understand, the difficulties and problems of your human relationships.

We know that problems arise and mistakes are made, for there is also that in every human being which is weak. When another slips up, and does or says something you think is wrong, remember, you do not know the whole truth, you only see a tiny aspect of the picture. You know neither the karma nor the weakness and temptation of another and therefore you cannot judge. We cannot judge, but we can all love, and all have to learn the meaning of love. Love is service to God. To love is to serve the God in your brother. Be true to God.

*

Now, withdraw into the temple of your heart.

Meditate on the perfect pink rose. The rose lies on the altar in the temple of the heart. Its petals are opening to the Sun – every petal living and glowing with light. And there is ineffable light in the heart of the rose.

Become enfolded in those petals, in soft pearly light. You are in the temple of the rose, the Sun pours down into the heart . . . the Sun is the Christ-being, all love. You are part of Him and one with all humanity, in the heart of the rose.

22

THE LAKE OF PEACE

PROBLEMS confuse you because you are bound down to the material level of thought and life. When you rise into the light of the Christ life, you are no longer confused; you are filled with knowledge, your way is certain, your body is healed. It is the chaos of the lower planes which limits you, and yet every soul can rise above this limitation. Hold the picture in your heart, for all time, of the Christ presence.

When you are in difficulties, when the problems of life press upon you and you are unable to see your way, and still less to make any decisions, be still, be tranquil in spirit as though you are seated on a summer's day beside a quiet lake. There is no hurry, remember, no hurry in the spiritual sense. Always be guided and directed by spiritual principles and laws. The true mason makes use of the working tools of his craft, in other words he applies spiritual principles to his daily life. When you too can do this you will find inner peace and surety, because you will have set in motion forces which will work constructively in your life and in your world.

*

Visualise the still waters of the lake of peace. There is no movement except a gentle lapping of the water on the margin of the lake. Meditate by the shore of the lake, and feel the cool, cleansing touch of the water upon your feet and hands and brow. All is so still . . .

There is a path of light across the surface of the water into the heart of the Sun . . . All that is of the earth in you, all that separates, is consumed in the light of the Sun.

Be still . . . in the Sun.

23

THE GRAIL TEMPLE

DO NOT be confused by words or the opinions of men. When the Lord Christ spoke through Jesus on earth he said that the pure in heart should see God. Not the man with the highly developed intellect, not the man of great book-learning, but the simple humble, loving son or daughter of God. This, my children, is the way and it is the *only* way into the secrets of creation, the secrets of eternal life. The power which comes to man in the secret chamber of his heart is the power which will feed man and help him to perceive the truth of life. So learn, my children, to go into the sacred silence of the grail temple and kneel before the altar and wait . . .

Perhaps you will see the great angel of the Sun with wings outstretched guarding the holy grail; and perhaps you will see the form of the gentle Christ standing with the grail cup before Him. And He will raise the cup to your lips and you will drink deeply. The golden liquid will flow all through your being, pulsating through every atom, the physical, mental and spiritual atoms of which you are composed.

*

We stand together in the healing temple of the Most High. The Great Spirit pours down upon you the golden rays from heaven . . . your cup, the grail cup which is your heart, is being filled, filled with the power of the spirit. Be filled with this balm . . .

We worship Thee. Infinite, boundless light and power and goodness, we surrender to Thee . . . May we be healed, cleansed, strengthened and perfected in Thy life . . .

24

BE STRONG IN THE LIGHT

ALL things are passing, and karma does not endure for ever.

When you look on human suffering, whilst you give sympathy, kindness and understanding, do not be dragged down by it. Do not allow your emotions to sweep you along like a piece of straw on the winds. Be still and look into the heart of the blazing Star. From the centre of this Star, the light and the strength of God your heavenly Father flow into your heart and your whole being, giving you a firm and straight backbone. Do remember to keep your back straight, not only physically but spiritually and mentally! We speak to some of you personally because we know you need courage, you need strengthening. Remember, everything passes, all things change, except

God, and God is within you. Your consciousness of God is daily increasing, and
this is all that matters – your expanding
consciousness of God who rules the kingdom which is your life.

*

Be still, and look into the heart of the Star . . .
See, in the heart of the Star a shining angel
form, the angel of the Star, with wings of light
outspread. You are enfolded in those wings of
light. The angel is so calm and still, remote from
earth yet all love. Be at peace. All is well.

25

LET GO FUTILE WORRIES

CAST out fear, my children. There is nothing for you to fear. Fear is a weakness, a chink in your armour of light; if you are fearful you are opening a way for the enemies, the adversaries of God. You weaken yourself when you give way to fears either for yourself or for others. Have no fear; place your whole confidence in God, your Father–Mother.

Your difficulty on earth is that you want things to hurry up, you want things to happen all at once; but spiritual power works slowly. If you put a seed or a bulb in the ground it won't be hurried, it will take its time to grow and eventually bloom. This is how spiritual power works.

If you live tranquilly and patiently, always with the consciousness of God's love upholding you, you will find that all your life will be heaven. Whatever has crept into and seemingly spoilt your life will all gradually be resolved. But this won't happen if you harbour irritation, fear and chaos in your own heart. Let go these futile worries and fears, my children. All things work together for good for him who loves God.

Your Father in heaven knows your need. Why be anxious? Seek the inner silence, the stillness of the pure spirit. In this shall your strength lie.

*

Rise, in spirit, into the sunlit garden – the infinite and eternal garden of the spirit. There are flowering shrubs, and many tiny perfumed flowers underfoot (your feet do not crush them as you walk). Among the many beautiful trees there is one especially, set beside the stream, which calls you; and you sit down, your back against the trunk. You feel the strength of the tree as you rest against it, and gradually you become absorbed

58

into its life, aware of its roots reaching down to draw strength and sustenance from mother earth, and its branches lifted towards the Sun, absorbing the life-force from the Sun and the air. You become aware of the flow of life from earth to heaven and heaven to earth, the inbreathing and the outbreathing. You become the tree . . . It is a tree of light, strong, steadfast, reaching towards the Sun, sheltering and succouring many beneath its branches of light.

26

LIFE IS NOT SOLEMN!

ALWAYS work for harmony. Know also that if you follow the true light, which is love, nothing can go wrong. Everything fits into place like the pieces of a jigsaw puzzle. *You* do the right thing. *You* obey the Law. God will do the rest. And remember a sense of humour will save many a little difficulty. Be amused! You will see the twinkling eye of the Master, and if you see White Eagle with clear vision you will see that we often have a twinkle in our eye.

Jesus, when on earth, enjoyed fun. Do you know, we would be happy to see you all dancing a divine dance! We do not want to see you with solemn faces; we like to see you merry, we assure you that brothers on our side of life are not long-faced. They have learnt to give joy to life, and in their giving they also become joy and happiness. In the brotherhood of ages past there was always to be found the spirit of happiness and fun; but remember, this brings wisdom and balance. It is so important to be balanced in your spiritual life. You may devote your life to spiritual service, but this doesn't mean a life of gloom. No – you radiate joy and light.

Now, we draw you all into the great Heart; remember that you are children of God and that all good flows from God.

And don't forget the twinkle in the eye, and kindness and tolerance!

*

You are in a small canoe gently floating on a still lake – floating along the path of light made by the Sun rising above the eastern hills. Seabirds are flying nearby, their outstretched wings catching the sunlight as they wheel along the air currents. You feel the urge to join them, and find that you too have wings. You stretch white wings

61

in the sunlight – feel the spirits of the air bearing you skywards, laughing, singing, revelling in the beauty of sky and earth and water. You are flying right into the heart of the Sun . . .

27

IF I BE LIFTED UP

WHEN the elder brethren come to you they do not come in grandeur, although you may see them in the blazing light because your spirit is open to their aura. You see them clothed in sunlight and they may appear as magnificent beings, but they are only magnificent because they are humble and gentle and pure. And when the master comes to you, he comes not in glory and in majesty, but as a brother whom you know well. He walks by your side as Jesus walked with his disciples on the road to Emmaus.

Jesus said: *He that believeth on me, the works that I do shall he do also.* Remember also, in the process of your development, that you must inevitably help others, for as you develop the Christ spirit within you, you are healing the sick, you are comforting the mourner, you are raising all humanity. *I, if I be lifted up* from the earth *will draw all men unto me.* What a wonderful future for you, and a glorious destiny!

May the peace of the spirit bless you.

*

We would draw for you a picture of the Master Jesus, warm in humanity, gentle, understanding you and your every need, your disappointments and your fears. Yet he is afire with the light of the Christ spirit and comes to you from the heart of the Sun with arms outstretched in giving and in surrender to God's will. Dwell on the human form of this perfect son—daughter of the living God, clothed in the white and gold rays of the Sun; focus this picture in your heart, dwell on it. Say in your heart 'Christ within me is the resurrection and the life . . .' and feel that life rising in you; feel the power of the light coursing through your whole being.

His power and love enfold you and raise you out of limitation into freedom.

28

THE SERENE AND TRANQUIL MIND

WE ADVISE you, beloved children, to learn the secret and the power of a tranquil and serene mind; to pray amid the turmoil of your earthly life for calmness of mind and heart. And when you have attained to a degree of calmness, you will not find it difficult to love.

In your outer life, in the outer courts, there is inharmony, harshness, noise and disturbing elements. But in the heart, the true temple of the spirit, there may always be peace, stillness and love.

We understand your individual difficulties, we know how hard it is for you to prevent the impatient 'mob' from invading your inner lodge. But this you have to learn to do. You have to retain the peace and sanctity of the lodge within, and so control the outer court that you can hear the voice of your master when he speaks. The master's voice is the Christ within your heart.

*

Withdraw into your inner world, to meditate beside the pool; enjoy the warm fragrance of the aromatic herbs growing between the stones which edge the pool.

You are in the company of gentle white-robed brethren who smile a welcome. One particularly draws you towards him. He is seated in the lotus posture, so calm and still, he radiates peace. You sit before him, as a child, meditating with him on the pure white lily lying so serene on the surface of the water, glowing with an inner light. As you meditate, you absorb from him ageless wisdom and deep peace.

29

THE SEED OF LIGHT

WHEN your heart is full of love and com-
passion you are sending out from your own
centre the light which God has implanted in
you as a tiny flame, which is growing all the
time. As you aspire to the Great White
Spirit, so this light and power is growing in
you. Every thought of God, every prayer to
God, every small effort that you make
to think rightly, to convey love to your
fellow beings, to reach up to the higher
level of harmony, love, purity and
goodness, is helping to heal the whole
world.

The work of the Brotherhood is to heal
the sick soul of the world, the sick soul of a
nation and the sick souls of men. To heal
sick bodies is good, but to heal the soul is
better. The quiet infiltration of this holy

light into men's hearts and lives, will heal the whole world.

Look beneath the outer mask of things, look beneath the outer mask of words. Seek the true spirit; help your brethren to do the same by your own acts.

*

The symbol given for meditation is the golden grain of corn, and the tiny flame of life enfolded in its protecting sheath. Meditate on the unfolding life in the seed as the roots reach down into the earth to find nourishment there; and the green blade rises towards the Sun to absorb the blessing of the Great Light.

Become at one with the flame within the seed; feel yourself to be that tiny grain of corn, and that the flame within you is reaching towards the Sun. Feel the creative stillness in the heart of the seed and let the growth of the light in you be for the blessing of all mankind.

30

YOUR POWER TO HELP THE WORLD

THE greatest service you can render to mankind is to work truly and earnestly on the inner plane to radiate love and establish on the physical plane of life the thought, the ideal, the feeling of brotherhood. Think often of the shining Star Brotherhood, the brotherhood of the light. They know no darkness, doubt or fear. They know that all is moving forward to ultimate brotherhood.

Never waver in your belief that all is working together for the good of humanity. In the measure that you hold fast to this truth, so will you increase your power to help the world and all humanity.

Keep on keeping on, although the hill seems insurmountable when you have to turn a corner and you cannot see the summit. Keep on persevering with your climb, knowing that the summit of that mountain is in the light of the sun, and that in due time all men will reach it.

Preserve in your heart the strength of the spirit of Christ; give forth good thought – love thought. Humanity will absorb the light that you send forth. Instead of absorbing the dark and the destructive forces, they absorb the Light, the constructive, the Godlike, the Christlike qualities of life.

*

Meditate on the still white flame in the heart of the Star, which will lead you into the temple of the Sun where they dwell, the shining Christ–Star-circle, who hold the earth and all her people in their care.

You too, your spirit, becomes part of this light of the Sun. You are not separate from them, or from any of God's creation. Say: I AM a flame in the heart of the Sun. I AM in the heart of the Sun.

31

SURRENDER TO GOD'S LOVE

IF YOU will contemplate for a moment the intricate beauty of the butterfly's wing, or the petals of a rose, you will perhaps begin to glimpse the perfect plan which is in the mind of your Creator; you will know that all is good, all is working in obedience to divine law. It will help you to understand the working of that law, and the wisdom that is behind the plan of your life, if we say that you have with you your guardian angel and your teacher, your individual master who knows and is part of you, who understands every thought and aspiration of your heart and mind.

A sparrow *shall not fall on the ground without your Father. But the very hairs of your head are all numbered.* When he said this Jesus was trying to convey how great is

God's love for you, His child. If you could only surrender yourself to God's law and understand that what is happening to you is all part of a perfect outworking of this law, you could then be at peace. There is no need for you to feel overburdened, fearful, or sad; it is only the lower mind which is irked and frustrated by conditions. The earthly mind is the enemy of the spirit, but you are learning that the spirit must be your master. If you think of these words you will realise that your master is your own spirit, and your own spirit is a part of the divine Master, the Son of God. Mastery over yourself, and over your life can only grow and develop in you by your obedience to the divine law of love.

As you seek the light by giving love and gentleness and kindness so you will find the light. The light is life.

*

Close the doors of your Lodge; shut out the world; still the outer, worldly mind . . .

Be still, emotions, and be the servant of divine spirit . . .

Be still, O mind, be still, and be the servant of divine mind . . .

Now, open your inner vision and see the form of the Master, the perfect man, clothed in the garment of light. His robe glistens with the colour of the Sun and he is bathed in gold. He draws close to you. Kneel, in spirit, and receive his blessing.

32

THE POWER WITHIN

THE elder brethren know only love and simplicity and sweetness of nature. They work under the guidance and power of the Son, whom in your western world you call the Christ spirit. The great ones of the Christ-circle descend to earth to stimulate in man and in earth itself his divine light. They come to help you realise that there is the power within you, within all the children of God, to become healers of men; a power which can open the gates of heaven for you and enable you to find your way into the world of light in full consciousness, so that you will be familiar with the world to which you go, before actually leaving the physical body.

With the development of the power of pure spirit within, you will learn how to go into the world of light at will, and once there will meet your master – see him as a living being, clothed in a body like your own, but of finer ether. You will receive from him (or possibly her) words of love, comfort, wisdom, understanding of your needs. You will be enveloped in the master's love. But before you can reach that point you will have to train yourself, discipline yourself, and you must start simply.

First of all, humility; become as a little child. Second, learn in all your human relationships to be gentle. The master is all love, all gentleness, all humility. Only he can take you through the gate into the world of heavenly light and perfect harmony, where you will experience that complete and perfect love for which your spirit longs in the wilderness of the world.

*

Visualise a delicate pink rose, perfect in form and colour, opening its petals to the spiritual Sun which falls upon it. Try to become en rapport *with that rose . . . Inhale the spiritual perfume and absorb the delicacy of its life, its aura . . .*

It will raise you far above the earth into a world of stillness, peace, love and truth.

Withdraw into the consciousness of the rose as often as you can. It is the symbol of the Christ life, the Christ sweetness and purity. Its fragrance will permeate your being and it will help you to live within the infinite love.

33

THE COMPANIONSHIP OF THE UNSEEN

DO NOT separate heaven and earth, but strive rather to draw men into closer relationship with heaven. Strive for increasing co-operation and interpenetration between the higher worlds and the earth.

If you will be steadfast on the path to which your feet have been guided by your older brethren, you will find the treasure of life, a never-ending stream of help and healing and happiness. We, your brothers and guides, are on the road by your side. Not one of you stands alone. You have only to ask in simple trust, and you shall receive; whatever you need, it shall be supplied. Your guide knows your innermost need and will comfort you and lead you into green pastures and beside still waters.

When you become depressed and fearful, there is no strength, no health in you. We know that the trials of the body can bring about depression and lowered vitality, but this lowered vitality and depression can be overcome by the spirit of joy and by the light of the spirit, which must be sought. The windows of the soul must be flung wide, every day, to let in the sunlight of God's love.

When the weaker human self stands on one side, then the divine mind takes over and can control and manipulate matter. Those who do not understand divine law say, 'A miracle has happened!' But miracles start, my brethren, in your own soul.

*

Now gently and peacefully feel that you are in the ray of the beautiful shining Star, so still, so peaceful. You are breathing in the light from that still white Star at the heart of the Sun. Your whole being is filled with light. The Star which is your real Christ-self is shining in your heart, growing brighter with each gentle breath. You become the Star . . . you are all light.

Divine light shines in me. Divine life permeates and heals every atom of my being.

34

FAITH IS . . . GOD

HOW blest we are in our communion and communication between our two worlds. When you are engulfed in the life of physical and material things a dark curtain hangs between you and heavenly scenes, heavenly visitors; and when we find it difficult to penetrate that heavy veil our hearts overflow with love for you all. If you will always make the effort to turn away from dark and negative things and look to the divine love, and to the company of the shining ones who come very close to help you, then you, of your own free will, will draw aside the veil and there will be no darkness between you and them.

You live and have your whole being encompassed by the glorious love which we call God.

To be aware of God is to possess faith.

Faith is beyond all factual knowledge Faith is . . . God; a closeness to God, an indestructible awareness of God, a voice in the heart which whispers, 'I am here, my child; I am by your side; I supply every need. My ways are wisdom and love'.

This great love is enfolding you, and so long as you are willing to be enfolded in this heart of love, it will hold you and give you sweetness and comfort and strength; it will give you inspiration to walk bravely on your allotted path; it will give you companionship, it will give you love and joy indescribable; and will in time reveal to you the glory of God's life.

*

Lift your heart now in worship and adoration towards the glorious Sun, giver of life. In the heart of the Sun, see and feel the beautiful form of the Great Healer, the master craftsman, pouring his love and blessing upon you and upon all humanity.

35

THE GIFT OF LIFE

EACH one of us, however long we have lived, not only in the physical body but down the ages from the very beginning, has been tenderly watched over, guarded, guided by the divine Love, and has reason to be deeply thankful. Always remember this, and as you have been brought to this present day through joy, sometimes through grief, so you will be guided and cared for all the days of your life. Remember too that through every experience your soul has absorbed wisdom. Every man, woman and child is absorbing wisdom, is expanding in spirit. What a wonderful gift is life!

Accept, brethren, accept all that comes to you, both of pain and joy. Accept all these experiences and try to realise that they are precious gifts, without which you could not become a perfect son or daughter of the living God.

Your brethren in spirit would assure you of their continued companionship and love, and the way you can help yourselves to realise their companionship is to keep your thoughts above the turmoil and the destructiveness of the lower mind and earthly thoughts. Live above the limited consciousness of earth. Our world and your world are so close, but you set them apart when you forget that you are spirit, and that you live in a world of spirit. Live always in the consciousness of a higher world, of light and beauty. In this way you help to quicken the vibrations of the whole planet.

*

In our meditation we enter the infinite and eternal garden and feel the presence and the love of the divine Mother. Everywhere we see stirrings of new life, the pale green shoots, the early spring flowers, so many of them yellow, with a golden cup at the centre.

In imagination we raise this cup to our lips, and sip the life-giving essence it contains. We are strengthened, healed and inspired, and filled with love and thankfulness for life with all its beauty; thankfulness for the heavenly garden in which we meditate and draw close to God; and thankfulness above all for the greatest gift of God to man — light, the divine spark, the seed of golden grain, infinite and eternal within our hearts.

36

THE GENTLE BROTHERS

WE COME to bring joy and hope, to raise you up from the hardness and roughness of earth's journey, and to carry you for a brief space into higher spheres of life. Using your heavenly imagination, come with us to the mountain top, and there, in the light of the Sun and the stillness and peace of the mountains, see with the vision of your spirit, the temple of life wherein walk brothers and sisters who have trod the self-same path as you, and who have learnt from experience to trust the wisdom and love of the Great White Spirit.

Look into the faces of the gentle brethren and you will see tranquillity and peace expressed. You will also see simplicity, and great strength and nobility of spirit in their bearing. And the grandeur of the collective spirit of the Brotherhood manifests in their temple; in the grace and beauty of its architecture, and in the colours which glow softly and according to the need of the soul.

By such beauty you will recognise the quality of the souls who meet in this temple. Try to catch from them the same spirit of calm and confidence; and as they transfer it to you, so you in turn can transfer it to those on earth who are confused and unhappy. You can impart to them the confidence which has been given to you by your brethren from the spirit.

*

In our meditation we find ourselves before the altar, which is ablaze with heavenly light, and take communion with the gentle company of Brothers whom we hear chanting the great AUM . . .

We are bathed in peace . . . peace . . . peace . . . peace . . .

37

THE ELDER BRETHREN

THINK often of the gentle spirit of the Master. Strive to think as he would have you think, to speak as he. He is not alone, for many of the elder brethren such as he are helping mankind, those who have gained mastery over the lower and baser self and are no longer enmeshed by the frailties of the flesh. Such as these are masters over every happening, small or great. Tranquil and serene, they radiate the light of the eternal Christ. In them no darkness lingers. They are transparent, no longer base metal but gold without dross. Their light reaches to, helps, sustains and comforts every lesser brother striving on the path.

And while you are striving, remember you work not for yourself alone; for your influence, your outer life, makes the world of men happier and better, and your inner life of prayer and striving affects the thoughts and souls of many others. To live thus is to live no longer for self.

*

Let us go into the infinite and eternal garden, where the love and beauty of God manifests in the perfection of nature and in the goodly company of gentle brothers of the spirit who come close to help us with the fragrant qualities of their souls. Let us see the blue sky overhead, and feel the soft carpet of spring flowers underfoot.

Now we rest on the grass, in the sunshine. We feel the glory of the Sun as the warm golden rays pour into our hearts, and we see, in the centre of the Sun, gradually taking form, the embodiment in human form of the love of God, Christ, all love. He appears almost as a great cross of light. We surrender, we give ourselves, our hearts, into this golden blessing . . .

38

HAVE NO FEAR

YOU should be joyful, my dear ones, even in the face of difficulties, knowing that these difficulties mean that you have arrived at the point where you can clear away your karma. Sorrow, trouble, loss – these are not cruelly inflicted upon you by an avenging God; they are just the working out of divine law, and an opportunity for you to take the next step forward on your path.

Therefore we say, accept and be thankful for your life. Whatever comes to you, see in it an opportunity, and be thankful to God.

We speak to you from the realms of spirit, and we speak truth. God is love. His methods may be inscrutable, nevertheless we, which includes you, accept His way as being wise and loving. There is nothing to fear! God tenderly cares for you and has appointed a guardian angel and helper in spirit to watch over and guide you. You may not be able yet to see the way ahead, but live in the consciousness of God and know that at the right time, when you are ready, the way will be shown to you.

*

We are bathed in the pure life-giving rays of the Christ Star. Peacefully we breathe in the light and feel it flowing through every cell of our being, releasing all frets and tensions of the outer self. We are becoming still under the Star. Strong rays enfold us in wings of light as our guardian angel draws close to our innermost being. We become stiller, more peaceful, as deep in the heart a clear flame arises, grows and illumines our whole consciousness with a quality of God, divine peace, strength, courage, heavenly wisdom, joy, love. The angel's wings raise us heavenwards and we are bathed, immersed, irradiated with that God-quality which we need, deep within our soul.

39

THE MASTER SOUL

WE SHOULD like you to think of a rainbow, that beautiful arc of colour. Water is the symbol of the soul; and even as the rainbow in the sky has the seven primary colours, so the soul contains the seven aspects of being.

Will you think of the Master as being like that perfect rainbow, with all the colours exactly balanced and perfect? The rainbow is the clothing of the Master, and when all these colours are blended perfectly, the pure white light is the result.

Again, we draw the symbol of the Sun, or the Christ light, shining upon the soul of man (which is the water element), and causing the breaking-up of the colours into the rainbow. Thus through the sunlight of Christ shining through the soul, the beautiful colours of the soul, of the perfect man, are seen.

Imagine the radiant ones who have attained to this state of life, always in this state of calm and serene service to humanity. Visualise the colours of their robes, and the light which shines from their countenance, the gentle touch, the graceful and perfect poise as they go about their work. Hear the music which emanates from their clothing, from their voice, from the very words they utter. Visualise their surroundings in the infinite and eternal garden, and see the sunlight and the rays of colour brought into the moving water, the playing fountains.

These servants of God who walk in the garden are brothers of yours, who come to you and mingle with your spirit. They touch your shoulder sometimes, and speak in your heart and head gentle and encouraging words; they bring peace, they bring power; they bring a love which is comprehensive, enfolding and unifying. This is the brotherhood of the spirit.

You are not shut away from this glorious Brotherhood that we describe to you; they will never intrude upon your wish for isolation, but if you open your heart and say 'come' they come, so joyously, and will never fail to do so.

*

Let us be still now, centred in the light – in the steadfast stillness of the rising Sun. In the heart of the Sun, we imagine a sparkling jewel, from which glorious colours shine. As we become stiller and stiller the colours take form. Great wings of light envelop us in the soft beautiful colours of blue, green, gold, amethyst, pink, silver. We are aware of colour, music and perfume, and yet absolute stillness . . .

Be still and know God, and the angels.

40

LEARN TO LISTEN

ON THE spiritual path there are many seeming contradictions. You will be told to be very careful and to think before you speak or act. Later on the path you will be told you must learn to act spontaneously, to be quick and wise on the spur of the moment. You are at present at the stage where you must learn to be very guarded, very careful in speech. The wise man learns so much through silence. You know the story of the wise old owl who sat on a tree and looked and listened? Learn to be wise and silent – to listen. You want to listen to the spirit world, to listen to the words of love spoken by your beloved in the beyond, by your guide, your teacher, and later, by your master. Learn then to listen first to people on the earth plane – give your whole attention to the one who is speaking to you; listen also to the sounds of the birds and the animals, the song of the wind in the trees, and the song of falling raindrops and of the rushing river. This is how the Red Indians were trained from childhood; and because they were so trained, they were able to hear not only physical sounds, but sounds *behind* those of earth, the sounds of the unseen world. They could distinguish the voices of their spirit guides and teachers; they could also hear the voices of the nature spirits. It is difficult for you in these noisy cities to hear anything of these, yet you must train yourself to listen.

*

Come through the gate into the beautiful garden of the spirit. Sit quietly beside the gently flowing stream. The Sun is shining and all is quiet and peaceful. Be very still in your spirit and listen deeply to all the small sounds of nature in this beautiful garden. Listen to the sound of the quietly flowing water . . . the sound of little creatures, the hum of the bees . . .

Listen to the song of birds, the soft movement of the wind among the branches . . .

If you listen even more deeply you will hear the inner sound of all life, the inner music of the flowers and trees, and the very breath of the earth, rhythmic and beautiful.

And deeper still, beneath all this music and movement, there is profound and utter silence . . . deep, deep silence and stillness. Listen to the silence.

Within the silence is the harmony of God.

41

COMMUNION IN GOD

IN SILENCE you enter the temple of your soul, and hold sweet communion with God.

All the truth and wisdom to which you have attained in your many lives on earth goes to build the temple of your soul, your higher self. When you enter the silence, when you withdraw from the clamour of the outer world of man and the outer world of your own mind, and enter into the deep, deep silence of your innermost, you are entering the temple of your own soul. And there you may hold holy communion, first of all with God – part of yourself – source of your life, source of all power and health and happiness. Then, when you have made that contact with God in the silence, you will find yourself in the presence of saints. Those saints are very often your own beloved friends, for they too have passed through a process of purification and enter the temple with you because they are part of you, even as you are part of them. They are part of God, for they are in God and God is in them. This is holy communion.

If you would commune with those you love, first seek communion with God in the temple of your soul.

Blessed are the pure in heart: for they shall see God. They shall know God. By this communion, my children, the very atoms of the physical body are raised to a spiritual level. This is spiritual law, the law that brings perfect life to man, eternal life, for there is no death in the Kingdom of God.

Peace be with you, and the blessing of the great silence . . .

*

Be still in mind and spirit, breathe gently and deeply, breathing in the stillness and peace which is from God. Let all the disquiets of the outer world fall away as you withdraw into the small white and gold temple within. On the altar of light, here in your innermost, burns the still white flame. Kneel before the flame, gaze upon it until you become the flame.

Its light fills your being and its radiance encompasses the whole earth . . .

42

YOU ARE SPIRIT

WITH every prayer of yours, every aspiration, your guide comes joyfully to help you.

If you remain positive in thought and prayer you attract those who are your true helpers and who will enable you to develop clear vision, a clear sense of spiritual things and of the spirit world to which you are so closely attached. But if you allow yourself to indulge in pessimistic thoughts you attract similar thoughts and influences to you.

You live in the spirit world but you are unaware of it. To achieve peace of mind, health of body and all you need for your earthly journey, you must constantly realise that you are spirit. So many people think of disease and aches and pains instead of thinking in terms of spirit. They feel it is impractical to think of higher things when there is so much suffering on the physical plane that needs to be put right. But the true mystic is really a practical person. Man must get his thoughts right. He must hold thoughts of the spirit life and of the harmony of that life. He must hold the thought of the perfect body, the body of health, radiant with light.

Try to conduct your life in the consciousness of the eternal life, of the perfection of life. God's will for man is perfection, health and harmony. But as God blesses man abundantly, so man, in his turn, must bless his fellow creatures with true love, Christ love. In giving, man is blessed and the spirit in him released from the bondage of materiality.

*

Visualise the blazing Star shining still, bright, but reflecting all the soft colours of the spectrum. This Star is just above your head, and you are held, enveloped, in light which is pouring down from it. Now visualise the pure white flame in your heart centre. Be very still in mind and heart as you gaze upon it . . . A ray from the Star reaches and touches the flame in your heart, the flame which is your pure spirit . . . the flame reaches up into the Star – the two gradually become one.

Rest in this consciousness.

43

THY WAY, NOT MINE

BE PATIENT, brethren. Your work is in the plan, and the plan will unfold when you yourself have learned wisdom; when you have been prepared, perhaps through extreme difficulties in your physical life, for the work you have to do. Your troubles and frustrations are all part of your preparation, all helping you to become a more receptive instrument for the power of the spirit. Obey your conscience, the word of God in your heart. Bear difficulties courageously, and never lose faith.

We have said throughout the years, 'keep on keeping on'. This is the magic phrase – steadfastness. Pursue your path in spite of obstacles and difficulties. Sometimes the tests come thick and fast until you feel that you have had quite a battering; as you get up from one test, down you go with another. Do not be discouraged by this, but keep on faithfully, trusting that divine love and law which will eventually bring truth and wisdom within yourself; for you learn, not through words, but through your reactions to the tests.

When you can kneel before the altar of your inmost being and say, 'Not my will, O Lord, but Thy will. I humbly accept,' then the strength will come to you; joy will light your life and you will see truth; you will see divine law working out in human life. And believe us, this vision of the divine law at work in human life, in spiritual evolution, brings indescribable happiness.

The brethren bless you and tenderly love you. Think of their love for you and it will help you upward. They know your need; the supply is limitless.

*

We visualise the symbol of the cross of light encircled by light. The cross is man himself in incarnation but held always in the circle of God's love. Try to feel that you are the cross, with arms outstretched in giving and in surrender to God's great love. As you do so you become aware of a perfect rose at the centre of the cross – your heart.

As you meditate, the rose grows in size and you are enfolded in its fragrance – you are within the temple of the rose; its walls are soft and translucent, shining with rose-tinged light. You are surrounded by your spirit brethren and supported by their love.

44

I AM IN GOD. GOD IS IN ME

THE love, the light in the heart is pure spirit, the seed of God; and human life must be guided by the spirit. You make your affairs so complicated with the little mind of earth. But goodness is so simple. Learn, my dear ones, to be guided by the spirit, which is the love within you.

The wise man allows nothing to disturb him. He cares neither for praise nor blame, nor does he grieve either for the living or for the dead. He knows that the divine law is just, perfect and true, and that that law must work out in every human life. So never grumble or be discontented with your lot. If you will train yourselves to accept your karma, realising that you have much to gain from it, you will be able to live so much more happily.

The most powerful instrument for help is prayer, used with sincerity and humility. Pray for one single thing, which is God's love; pray for an increase of God's light, not only for yourself but in order that others may benefit and be blessed. Pray for God, pray for good, and resign all to God.

*

Now, relax mind and body and breathe quietly, slowly, deeply. As you breathe in, try to imagine that you are breathing in light and life; that you are not only inhaling air, you are filling every particle of your being with God's breath, with God's love, with light. As this love fills your heart and your mind, every atom, every cell of your body will be filled with perfect life. Repeat the words:

I am in God. God is in me.

45

THE HEALING MAGIC

IT IS a temptation for man to hug to himself a sense of guilt for past errors, perhaps even from a previous incarnation. But do not retain any guilt, remember instead the love of God, the mercy of God. Give yourselves in loving submission to your Creator, and be filled with divine love.

When you can accept the law of karma humbly and without resentment, then the power of the spirit begins to recreate first the soul and then the body; because true healing starts where all sickness starts – that is, in the soul. Healing power is released by love.

This is the core of healing magic. Deep, deep healing rises from the heart of the child of God, and it is love in the human heart – love for God, the Great White

Spirit – that heals, that brings peace of heart.

Forget, if you can, your physical body. Leave all and follow me, said the Master, and he is saying it still . . . Leave all and follow me. It sounds so simple but it is one of the most difficult things for earthly people to do. Look up. Look into the light. The light is always there but the mind and the emotions of man blindfold him and separate him from the consciousness of God. All life is God, and when a man can leave the entanglements of the earthly self and dwell in the consciousness of the eternal good, he is immediately in heaven. He knows no limitation. In spirit there is neither pain nor disease because spirit is perfect, spirit is at one with God, is part of God.

*

Now, leave the entanglements of your mind and your physical conditions, shut out all discordancy and doubt and fear, and rise into the world of light. Turn your face towards the Sun, the warm gentle sunlight. Breathe in this light . . . it is the life of God, the life which will make you whole. You are spirit, perfect in God.

I am perfect as my Father created me perfect. I am divine love . . . I am divine peace.

LIFE IN THE SUN

WE WOULD raise your consciousness now to a life which every soul has once known in the sphere of the Sun. From the Sun we all come, to the Sun we all return. Is there not an answering echo in your innermost being when we speak of the Sun-sphere? You make the mistake of thinking of the Sun or the Christ-sphere only as something towards which you are travelling – which is true in one way, for it is indeed a state of consciousness towards which you are moving. But understand also that it is a state of life from which you have come, and in moments of exaltation you can, very faintly, glimpse the glory of the Sun or the Christ-sphere. It is only a vague hope maybe, but you can still understand that such a condition of life exists. It would seem that the spirit has travelled far, far away, since it first came forth from God, but has never wholly lost the true consciousness of its Source, for in times of dire need, the soul will reach out to its God, its Creator. The very yearning towards God is indicative of the life of God or the universal Sun which dwells within man's being.

God said, Let there be light: and there was light; and from that light everything was created. From that light we have come; to that light we return, ourselves beings of light, rich in experience, having gained wisdom, love and power, having grown, at the end of that journey, to the full stature of the son–daughter of God – complete, perfect.

*

Let us meditate on a state of life which is wholly in the Sun, in the light. We are raised in spirit into realms far, far beyond the earth. We find ourselves being taken into a disc of light like a blazing Sun. We are carried into the very heart of this glorious light of the Sun. This is eternal life, the life from which we have come, the life to which we are returning. As we meditate within this Sun-life, we begin to become aware of the perfected ones, the perfect life; we are truly looking through the gate of heaven into the world of Christ.

Now we see man as the cross, radiating light, until the cross becomes absorbed into light, and all that remains is the Sun, the Christ.

May the rays of the Sun fill your whole being, that you may be healed and strengthened and illumined by the power of Christ.